W9-BWI-222

JOE FLACCO and the Baltimore Ravens

SUPER BOWL XLVII

by Michael Sandler

Consultant: Charlie Zegers
Football Expert and Consultant for *Basketball Heroes Making a Difference*

BEARPORT
PUBLISHING

New York, New York

Credits
Cover and Title Page, © Elise Amendola/AP Images; 4, © Tom Croke/Icon SMI; 5, © John Angelillo/UPI/Newscom; 7, © Getty Images; 9, © Pamela Kay Schmalenberger/AP Images; 10, © Richard C. Lewis/Icon SMI; 11, © Aaron Josefczyk/Icon SMI; 13, © Zumapress/Icon SMI; 15, © Tom Croke/Icon SMI; 16–17, 18, 19, © Zumapress/Icon SMI; 20, © Jeff Lewis/Icon SMI; 21, © Anthony J. Causi/Icon SMI; 22R, © Jeff Lewis/Icon SMI; 22L, © Anthony J. Causi/Icon SMI.

Publisher: Kenn Goin
Editor: Lisa Wiseman
Creative Director: Spencer Brinker
Design: Debrah Kaiser

Library of Congress Cataloging-in-Publication Data

Sandler, Michael, 1965–
  Joe Flacco and the Baltimore Ravens : Super bowl XLVII / by Michael Sandler ; Consultant, Charlie Zegers.
      pages cm. — (Super bowl superstars)
  Includes bibliographical references and index.
  ISBN-13: 978-1-61772-933-1 (library binding)
  ISBN-10: 1-61772-933-7 (library binding)
 1. Flacco, Joe—Juvenile literature. 2. Football players—United States—Biography—Juvenile literature. 3. Quarterbacks (Football)—United States—Biography—Juvenile literature. 4. Baltimore Ravens (Football team)—Juvenile literature. 5. Super Bowl (47th : 2013 : New Orleans, La.)—Juvenile literature. I. Title.
  GV939.F555S26 2014
  796.332092—dc23
  (B)

                                            2013011637

For more information, write to Bearport Publishing Company, Inc., 45 West 21st Street, Suite 3B, New York, New York 10010. Printed in the United States of America.

10 9 8 7 6 5 4 3 2 1

★ Contents ★

Third Try

Baltimore Ravens quarterback Joe Flacco had almost reached the Super Bowl twice. Both times, his team lost in the **AFC** Championship Game. On January 20, 2013, however, Joe had another chance. A victory against the New England Patriots in the AFC Championship Game would send Baltimore to Super Bowl XLVII (47).

Pulling off a win wouldn't be easy, however. The game was being played in New England. The Patriots had never lost a championship game at home. For Joe and his teammates, a huge challenge lay ahead.

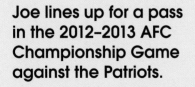

Joe lines up for a pass in the 2012–2013 AFC Championship Game against the Patriots.

The game against New England was the biggest challenge of Joe's career.

Joe and the Ravens had played in the AFC Championship Game in 2008–2009 and 2011–2012. The championship game decides which AFC team will play in the Super Bowl.

Learning the Game

Joe learned the game of football growing up in Audubon, New Jersey. He practiced passing the ball with his four younger brothers. "All four of us . . . were his first **receivers** ever," recalled his brother John.

The Flacco kids loved sports. They especially liked throwing footballs, shooting hoops, and hitting baseballs.

Joe, the oldest, **excelled** at just about every sport. Throwing a football, however, was his special talent. He was such a good player that his high school coach, Ralph Schiavo, believed he had the skills to make it to the **NFL**.

In high school, Joe was a star player in three sports: baseball, basketball, and, of course, football.

Today, Joe (back row, center)
is still close with his parents,
his four brothers, and his sister.

Delaware Star, Baltimore Starter

After high school, Joe attended the University of Delaware, where he became the school's star quarterback. He wowed his coaches and classmates with his incredibly strong arm and his **accurate** passes. He was certainly headed to the NFL, but to which team?

On **draft** day in 2008, Joe found out. He received a call from Baltimore's **GM**. "Hey, Joe," he said. "Are you ready to be a Raven?"

Baltimore wanted Joe to start his **rookie** year as a **backup** quarterback. However, when the other Ravens quarterbacks got hurt, the plan changed. Joe would be the team's **starter** from his very first game.

Baltimore drafted Joe in the first round of the 2008 NFL draft.

Joe set 20 school records for passing at the University of Delaware.

A Coach's Challenge

At first, Joe struggled against the big and talented NFL **defenders**. In his first five games, he threw seven **interceptions** and just one touchdown pass. The Ravens were struggling. They needed more from their quarterback.

After a terrible 31–3 loss to the Indianapolis Colts, **offensive coordinator** Cam Cameron turned to Joe. "You have to lead us," he said.

Joe stepped up to the challenge. In the next game, he completed 17 of 23 passes in a huge win over the Miami Dolphins. It was a turning point for the Ravens. They went on to win eight of their next ten games and rolled into the **playoffs**.

Joe looks to pass the ball in the winning game against the Miami Dolphins.

During the 2008–2009 season, Joe became the first rookie quarterback in NFL history to win two playoff games. Only a loss to the Pittsburgh Steelers in the AFC Championship Game kept Baltimore out of the Super Bowl.

Joe quickly lines up a pass before being tackled by a Pittsburgh Steeler.

The Ravens' Rising Star

After the 2008–2009 playoffs, Joe was seen as one of the NFL's rising stars. Over the next four seasons, he continued to play well. He won more games than any other quarterback, and helped Baltimore reach the playoffs each year.

Joe was lucky to be surrounded by talented teammates who played a big role in the team's success. For example, the Ravens had star **running back** Ray Rice. They also had a rock-solid **defense** built around Ray Lewis, Ed Reed, and Terrell Suggs.

Despite the team's success, Joe wanted more. He dreamed about a trip to the Super Bowl! In January 2013, after two playoff victories, a win over the Patriots would get him what he wanted.

Playoff wins against the Indianapolis Colts and the Denver Broncos sent the Ravens into the 2012–2013 AFC Championship Game against New England.

Joe threw for 282 yards (258 m) and two touchdowns in a 24–9 playoff win against the Indianapolis Colts.

Moving Past the Patriots

The AFC Championship Game against the Patriots didn't start off well for Baltimore. By halftime, a Ravens win seemed unlikely. Baltimore was losing, 13–7. Patriots quarterback Tom Brady had never lost at home when his team led at the half. Joe, however, didn't let Tom's record scare him.

First, Joe finished an 87-yard (80 m) touchdown **drive** with a perfect throw to **tight end** Dennis Pitta. He followed it up with two more touchdown throws, both to receiver Anquan Boldin. Meanwhile, Ray Lewis and the Ravens defense shut down Tom and the Patriots.

At game's end, Baltimore had outscored New England at home, 28–13. The Ravens were headed to Super Bowl XLVII (47) to face the San Francisco 49ers.

Dennis Pitta (#88) catches a pass in the AFC Championship Game against the Patriots.

In the Ravens' three playoff wins leading up to the 2013 Super Bowl, Joe threw eight touchdown passes without a single interception.

A Super Beginning

The 49ers were a very fierce **opponent**. Not only were they unbeaten in five Super Bowl appearances, but they had their own **dynamic** quarterback, Colin Kaepernick. To win, Joe would need to play the best football of his life.

Right from the start, the Baltimore quarterback threw perfect passes. His first quarter touchdown throw to Anquan Boldin gave Baltimore a 7–0 lead. Soon, he found Dennis Pitta for a second touchdown. Then, just before the half's end, Joe lofted a strong throw to receiver Jacoby Jones. Jacoby pulled it down for a 56-yard (51 m) touchdown. The Ravens were on a roll. They led 21–6 at the half.

49ers coach Jim Harbaugh is the younger brother of Ravens coach John Harbaugh. The game was the first brother vs. brother coaching matchup in Super Bowl history.

Joe (#5) completed 13 of 20 passes in the first half of Super Bowl XLVII (47).

Blackout

The second half started off just as strongly for the Ravens. Jacoby Jones returned the kickoff 108 yards (99 m) for a touchdown. With a 28–6 lead, the Ravens were headed for a **blowout** victory.

Then the unimaginable happened—a power failure in the stadium caused the lights to go out. It was dark for a half hour, causing play to stop. When the lights finally came back on, San Francisco took over the game.

First, Colin Kaepernick threw a touchdown pass. Then, running back Frank Gore ran for another score. Finally, David Akers kicked a field goal. With 17 quick points, the 49ers had chopped the lead to 28–23. This game was no longer a blowout!

Jacoby Jones's (#12) 108-yard (99 m) kickoff return set a Super Bowl record.

Baltimore Ravens players wait for play to begin again after a power failure caused the lights to go out during Super Bowl XLVII (47).

No team had won a Super Bowl after falling behind by ten points or more. If San Francisco came back to win, they would make history.

Champions!

San Francisco had turned the game around. Joe, however, wasn't going to let victory slip away. He calmly led Baltimore on a 12-play drive, which kicker Justin Tucker finished with a field goal.

When Colin struck back with a 15-yard (14 m) touchdown run, Joe responded again. He led Baltimore downfield for another field goal. It was all the Ravens needed. Their defense held off the 49ers. When the game ended, Baltimore had a 34–31 win. Joe and the Ravens were Super Bowl champions!

Justin Tucker (#9) kicks a field goal in the second half of Super Bowl XLVII (47).

Joe was named **MVP** of Super Bowl XLVII (47). He completed 22 of 33 passes for 287 yards (262 m) and 3 touchdowns.

Joe celebrates both the Super Bowl XLVII (47) win and being named MVP of the game.

★ Key Players ★

There were other key players on the Baltimore Ravens who helped win Super Bowl XLVII (47). Here are two of them.

★ Jacoby Jones #12

Position: Wide Receiver

Born: 7/11/1984 in New Orleans, Louisiana

Height: 6' 2" (1.88 m)

Weight: 220 pounds (100 kg)

Key Plays: Scored two touchdowns—a 56-yard (51 m) pass from Joe Flacco and a record-breaking 108-yard (99 m) kickoff return

★ Anquan Boldin #81

Position: Wide Receiver

Born: 10/3/1980 in Pahokee, Florida

Height: 6' 1" (1.85 m)

Weight: 220 pounds (100 kg)

Key Plays: Caught six passes for 104 yards (95 m), including a first-quarter touchdown that gave Baltimore the lead

★ Glossary ★

accurate (AK-yuh-ruht) precise; on target; free from mistakes

AFC (AY-EFF-SEE) letters standing for American Football Conference; one of the two conferences in the National Football League (NFL)

backup (BAK-uhp) a player who doesn't play at the start of a game

blowout (BLOH-out) a game in which one team scores many more points than the other team

defenders (di-FEN-durz) players who try to stop players on another team from scoring

defense (di-FENSS) the part of a team that has the job of stopping the other team from scoring

draft (DRAFT) the event in which pro teams take turns choosing college players to play for them

drive (DRIVE) a series of plays that begins when a team gets the ball

dynamic (dye-NAM-ik) energetic, powerful; able to have a great effect on games

excelled (ek-SELD) performed very well

GM (JEE-EM) letters standing for General Manager; the person who chooses the players for a team

interceptions (in-tur-SEP-shuhnz) passes that are caught by players on the defensive team

MVP (EM-VEE-PEE) letters standing for Most Valuable Player, an award given to the best player in a game or in a season

NFL (EN-EFF-ELL) letters standing for the National Football League, which includes 32 teams

offensive coordinator (aw-FEN-siv koh-WAR-duhn-ay-tur) the coach in charge of a team's offensive players and plans for scoring points

opponent (uh-POH-nuhnt) a team that another team tries to beat in a sporting event

playoffs (PLAY-awfss) the games held after the regular season ends to determine a league's champion

receivers (ri-SEE-vurs) players whose job it is to catch passes

rookie (RUK-ee) a player who is in his first year of NFL football

running back (RUHN-ing BAK) a player who carries the ball on running plays

starter (START-ur) a person who plays at the start of a game; the best player at a position

tight end (TITE END) an offensive player who lines up next to a tackle, blocks for running backs, and catches passes as a receiver

Bibliography

Hagen, Paul. "Flacco a Leading Factor in Ravens' Success." *The Philadelphia Daily News* (January 15, 2009).

Samuel, Ebenezer. "Super Bowl XLVII: For Baltimore Ravens QB Joe Flacco, a New Jersey Native, Sports Run in the Family." *New York Daily News* (January 31, 2013).

Tresolini, Kevin. "Ravens Make Trade to Grab UD Star Flacco." *Wilmington News Journal* (April 27, 2008).

Read More

Frisch, Aaron. *The Story of the Baltimore Ravens (NFL Today)*. Mankato, MN: Creative Education (2010).

Krumenauer, Heidi. *Joe Flacco*. Hockessin, DE: Mitchell Lane (2010).

Sandler, Michael. *Joe Montana and the San Francisco 49ers: Super Bowl XXIV (Super Bowl Superstars)*. New York: Bearport (2009).

Learn More Online

To learn more about Joe Flacco, the Baltimore Ravens, and the Super Bowl, visit **www.bearportpublishing.com/SuperBowlSuperstars**

Index